FOUR STEPS TO KISS YOUR LIFE

Simple Methods to Dwell

in Happiness

Karthik

Chengalvarayan

Dedication

This book is dedicated to my wife, Revathy Cassilingam, the bravest lady I know.

Acknowledgements

I would like to acknowledge the enormous help given to me in creating this book. I wish to thank the author of 'Show Your Work' Austin Kleon, for reimaging my thoughts to build confidence in writing this book.

Also, special thanks to my wife and daughter, who often believe in me more than I do myself.

Also, special thanks to Monica-Writers of USA, and my editor for handling this project with just the right touch.

About Karthik

Karthik Chengalvarayan is a technical lead in the IT Industry with a wild passion for reading.

He is currently immersing himself in habit-forming techniques for well-being. Having lived in 4 different countries, he has always been passionate about understanding and respecting each culture.

Karthik lives in Canton, Georgia, with his beautiful wife, daughter and son.

Contents

INTRODUCTION

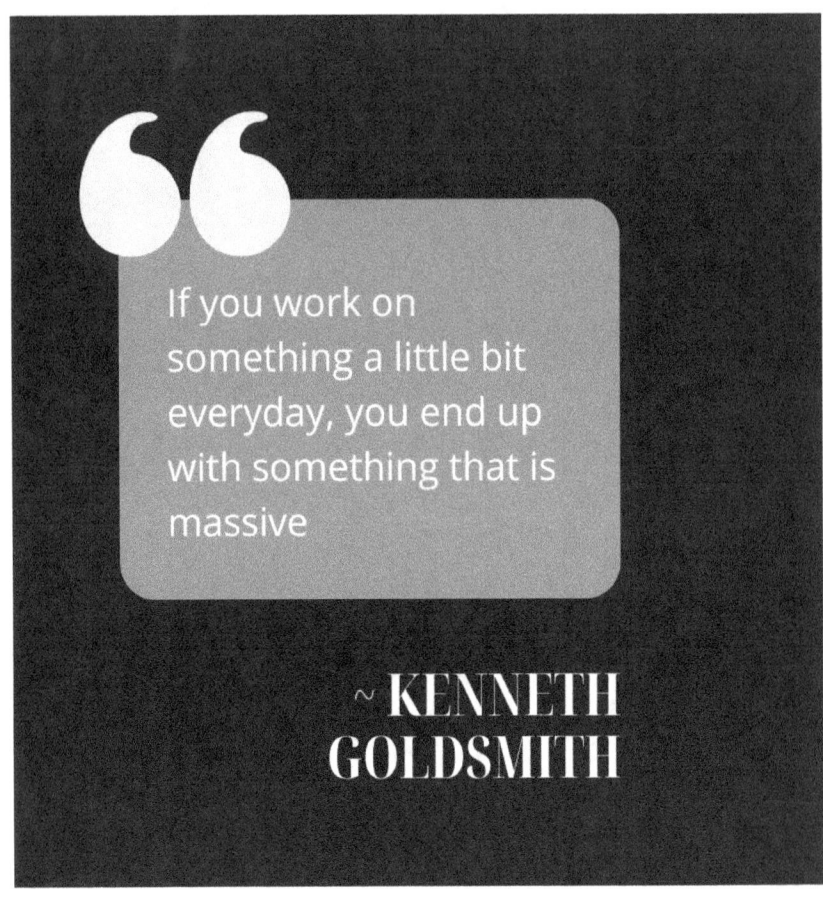

> If you work on something a little bit everyday, you end up with something that is massive

~ **KENNETH GOLDSMITH**

Welcome to the world of self-help literature, where countless voices stream with promises of transformation and enlightenment. You may find yourself pondering the age-old question: *"Why should I choose this book among the many?"* Allow me to offer a straightforward response: because, like you, I was once faced with the pursuit of a more meaningful and fulfilling life. Through a series of seemingly modest yet profoundly impactful habits, I unearthed a path that reshaped my existence, compelling me to share these discoveries with you.

Hailing from the heartland of India and navigating the streets of life, I eventually found myself in the bustling landscapes of the United States, drawn by the promise of opportunity and growth. While my name may not be a part of bestseller lists, and this book marks my foundational foray into the world of authorship, I am steadfast in my belief that the power of a first work lies not in its praises, but in its raw authenticity and unrestrained passion.

Consider the timeless wisdom of *"The Alchemist"* by Paulo Coelho or *"The Monk Who Sold His Ferrari"* by Robin Sharma—both seminal works that continue to inspire generations with their fresh perspectives and transformative insights.

Within the pages of *"4 Steps to Kiss Your Life,"* I extend to you an invitation—an invitation to embark on a journey of self-discovery, guided by the lessons gathered from my own personal story. I make no grand claims of wealth or worldly success, nor do I profess to hold all the answers. Instead, I stand before you as a humble seeker, navigating the ebbs and flows of life with an unwavering commitment to growth and self-improvement. Together, we will explore the intricacies of health, the depths of relationships, and the pathways to prosperity, armed with practical insights and actionable strategies designed to propel you toward a life of fulfillment and purpose.

As you move forward with me, I encourage you to approach these pages with an open heart and a curious mind, ready to embrace the transformative power of possibility and embark on a journey of self-discovery unlike any other. For within the depths of our shared experiences lie the seeds of limitless potential, waiting to be nurtured and cultivated into the vibrant medley of a life well lived.

KICK OFF YOUR MORNING

> **Every day, now is an extra day.**
>
> ~ GEORGE LUCAS

It's a familiar tale: the fresh promises of a new year, the resolutions made with passion, only to fade into the background as days pass by. We've all been there, grappling with the challenge of forming new habits, only to find ourselves faltering and drifting away from our intentions.

So, how do we break this cycle? How do we truly commit to change? The answer lies in the simple act of starting. To cultivate a new habit, we must take that initial step, and more importantly, we must commit to starting and ending each day with purpose and consistency.

For many, the first step on this journey is the daunting task of waking up early—"beating the sun," as they say.

It's no secret that rising with the dawn is a formidable challenge. The allure of the snooze button signals, and before we know it, those extra two hours slip away, leaving us to begrudgingly greet the day at our usual hour.

If the person normally wakes up at 7 am, and decides to wake at 5 am is not easy. I know many people do the snooze for years and still wake up late.

I, too, found myself trapped in this cycle of inconsistency. Despite my best efforts and suggestions gathered from websites, YouTube, and motivational quotes, I struggled to embrace the dawn with open arms.

Yet, amidst the haze of failed attempts, one desire burned brightly within me: the yearning to greet the early hours of the morning, when the world lay slumbering around me—my wife and children included. It was a time ripe with potential. This is the best time to unleash my creativity, strengthen my body, or simply revel in the blissful solitude of "ME" time.

During this period, I stumbled upon a book called 'The 5 AM Club' by Robin Sharma. Little did I know, it would become a catalyst for a profound transformation in my life. The real magic didn't lie in the act of waking up at 5 AM itself, but rather in the profound inspiration and influence the book imparted upon me.

Now, I won't claim that reading 'The 5 AM Club' magically turned me into a 5 AM riser overnight. It was just one piece of the puzzle. Alongside the insights gleaned from the book, I also made some simple yet impactful investments in tools and practices that helped solidify this new habit.

Here are three of them:

Old School Alarm Clock - $12: Sometimes, the simplest solutions are the most effective. I invested in a classic, no-frills alarm clock—one that doesn't take no for an answer. Its persistent beeping is enough to rouse even the heaviest of sleepers, ensuring I don't hit that snooze button and drift back into slumber.

Vision Board - $23: A vision board serves as a visual reminder of my goals and aspirations. It's a collage of images, quotes, and affirmations that inspire and motivate me to seize the day. Each morning, as I glance at my vision board, I'm reminded of the reasons behind my early wake-up call, fueling my determination to make the most of each day. I write tasks on the board and check them out once I've accomplished them.

Self-Talk - $0: Perhaps the most powerful tool in my arsenal doesn't cost a dime. It's the practice of self-talk—the art of consciously guiding my thoughts and beliefs towards positivity and empowerment. Through gentle affirmations and encouraging words, I reinforce the belief that I am capable of achieving my goals, one morning at a time.

But beyond the tools, what truly propelled me forward was a shift in mindset. I began to view each morning as an opportunity—a chance to set the tone for the day ahead, to carve out time for self-care, growth, and reflection. As I embraced the quiet solitude of the early hours, I discovered a newfound sense of clarity and purpose, allowing me to approach each day with renewed vigor and enthusiasm.

I kept the alarm clock out of my reach in the corner of the room. To switch off the alarm in the morning, you must wake walk for a few feet to stop. This worked like a charm. Tough for a few days, and autopilot after a few weeks.

I write this one task, 'wake up early' before the night and strike out in the morning; this board sits straight to my eye contact in my office room. If I missed that day of waking up, I feel guilty while seeing it. This pushed me to wake next day instead of feeling guilty again.

I do self-talk when I hear the alarm. Do you want the day to be successful or unsuccessful? This is another push to fight with your brain to win. Remember, if you wake up before 5.03 am, you win. But if you go for the next snooze at 5.15 am, your mind says you have already lost the battle. Your inner thought teaches you that you are already late to wake up and continue to enjoy. Your mind wins, and your body slumps. Then, another day of guilty for not doing what you planned.

These simple techniques gradually transformed waking up early from a mere habit into a lifestyle—a cornerstone of my daily routine. In addition to the tools and practices I've mentioned, here are a few more tips that have proven invaluable on my journey:

Additional Tips

Sometimes, you need to give yourself a strong incentive to wake up. Consider self-bribing as a strategy. For example, if you're a coffee lover, remind yourself that a steaming cup of coffee awaits you. Or if you enjoy nature walks, let that be your motivation. These cues serve as gentle reminders of the rewards that await you when you rise with the dawn.

But amidst all the tips and resources, one truth reigns supreme: the power of belief. Habit change begins with you. Reserve space in your mind or jot down your intentions in a note—what will you do during these early hours? Whether it's tackling important work tasks, dedicating time to your business, or indulging in some well-deserved "ME" time like reading, walking, or working out, having a plan in place sets the stage for success.

Keep in mind, that the early hours offer a unique opportunity for productivity and creativity. Your body is refreshed, your mind rejuvenated. Studies show that you can be up to 200% more productive during these early hours compared to the typical 9 to 5 grind. It's a time when solutions to long-standing problems emerge effortlessly, when clarity reigns supreme, and when progress feels within reach.

In the end, it wasn't about the hour on the clock, the tools at my disposal, or the additional tips. It was about reclaiming control of my time and my life—about prioritizing my well-being and committing to a journey of self-discovery and personal growth. As I continue to embrace the magic of the early hours, I'm reminded that true transformation begins with a single decision—a decision to rise and greet the dawn, ready to embrace the endless possibilities that lie ahead.

I could go on and on about the countless benefits of embracing the miracle of the morning, but I'd rather you experience them for yourself. Trust me—once you taste the sweet fruits of early rising, it becomes less of a chore and more of a pleasure. It's a shift that transforms not only your mornings but your entire outlook on life.

INTENSE PUSH

> " If you want to master the habit, the key is to start with repetition, not perfection.

~ JAMES CLEAR, AUTHOR OF ATOMIC HABITS

Every year, the gym sees a surge of hopeful individuals, determined to embark on their fitness journey. Yet, despite the initial enthusiasm, only a mere 5% manage to transform their resolutions into enduring habits. So, what sets these determined few apart from the rest?

What 95 % of people fall short? Yes, they also want to be in shape, lose weight, be healthy, and not suffer from chronic diseases in the future. But where is the gap? Because they are buried with excuses.

Excuses come from every corner…

The desire to prioritize health and fitness is widespread, yet many find themselves trapped in a web of excuses. The day may start with I need to send my kids to school; I couldn't continue because of my workload in the office; I got a knee and back pain, and I am tired in the evening, etc.

The morning rush, office deadlines, and physical discomforts all serve as convenient barriers to sidestep the commitment to exercise. Excuses are like, "You are busy driving, so you don't have time to fill the gas." You will be broken in the middle of the forest, where you won't find a gas station for the next 50 miles.

But amidst these obstacles lies a fundamental truth: the 5% who succeed face the same challenges as everyone else. What sets them apart is their unwavering commitment to prioritize their health above all else. Their priority of the work they planned is more important than giving excuses.

Consider this: we all have the same 24 hours in a day. It's how we choose to utilize this time that defines our priorities. Excuses, no matter how convincing, ultimately serve as self-imposed limitations—barriers that hinder our progress and suppress our potential.

Take, for example, the phenomenon of unused gym memberships. Many individuals eagerly sign up for year-long subscriptions, enticed by the appeal of discounted rates. Yet, come year-end, these memberships remain largely untouched, leaving individuals with little to show for their investment. It's a stark reminder that mere intentions without action amount to nothing.

I know 100's of people who took membership for an entire year at an offer price of $100. At the end of the year, they might have used 2 classes in a whole year. This is not the offer price. Technically, you paid $50 per session, which is very expensive, and you got nothing out of it.

Here are some tips to kickstart your fitness journey:

Invest in a Personal Trainer: It's a one-time investment that pays off in knowledge and guidance. While it may seem like an additional expense, the knowledge and guidance they provide can prove invaluable in navigating the complexities of fitness.

Learn the Basics: Fitness is like math—you can't tackle calculus without understanding numbers. Just as you wouldn't attempt calculus without understanding basic arithmetic, embarking on a fitness journey requires a foundational understanding of exercise principles.

Physical fitness is not just putting extra pressure on your body. It's an art you must learn for a lifetime, more importantly, to learn not to get injured.

Avoid Injury: Discomfort is normal, but learn to recover properly to avoid setbacks. It's also crucial to recognize that discomfort and setbacks are a natural part of the process. Injuries and muscle soreness may occur, but it's how we respond and recover from these setbacks that truly define our journey.

Find Motivation: Finding motivation is another key component of success. Excitement fuels consistency. Personal reflection helps you prioritize. Reflect on what drives you and prioritize accordingly. Remember, consistency is key—habits are formed through repetition, and it takes approximately 21 days for a behavior to become ingrained.

Stick to It: Consistency breeds habit. After 21 days, it becomes second nature. If you are a beginner, it's worth spending money on a personal trainer. It's a one-time investment but worth it.

Finally, choose a workout regimen that excites and motivates you. The whole industry has different flavors; whether it's the camaraderie of a boot camp class or the rhythm of a Zumba session, find what speaks to you and embrace it wholeheartedly. Never stop because of the reason it's expensive. It's an investment in your body. ROI is being in shape, active, and healthy.

Your monthly bills on OTT, Amazon, and restraints are way more expensive than a gym membership. But the benefits to your body are predominantly higher than other bills.

Engaging in early morning workouts yields a multitude of benefits that extend far beyond physical fitness. These benefits encompass various aspects of life, enriching both mind and body.

Enhanced Life Experience: Incorporating early morning workouts into your routine can significantly enhance your overall life experience. By starting your day with physical activity, you set a positive tone for the hours ahead. The sense of accomplishment and vitality gained from early morning exercise can permeate every aspect of your life, infusing each moment with renewed energy and purpose.

Improved Concentration: Engaging in physical activity in the morning primes your mind for optimal concentration throughout the day. Exercise stimulates the release of neurotransmitters such as dopamine and serotonin, which are associated with improved mood and cognitive function. As a result, you may find yourself more focused, alert, and productive in your daily endeavors.

Enhanced Decision-Making: Regular exercise has been shown to enhance cognitive function and decision-making skills. By kickstarting your day with a workout, you prime your brain for optimal performance, enabling you to make clearer, more decisive choices throughout the day. The clarity of mind gained from early morning exercise empowers you to navigate challenges with confidence and resilience.

Heightened Energy Levels: One of the most noticeable benefits of early morning workouts is the surge in energy levels experienced throughout the day. Exercise stimulates the release of endorphins, natural mood elevators that promote feelings of vitality and well-being. By harnessing the invigorating power of early morning exercise, you can banish feelings of lethargy and embrace each day with enthusiasm and vigor.

Enhanced Mood and Well-Being: Engaging in physical activity triggers the release of endorphins, neurotransmitters that are often referred to as "feel-good" chemicals. These endorphins promote feelings of happiness, reduce stress levels, and alleviate symptoms of anxiety and depression. By incorporating early morning workouts into your routine, you cultivate a sense of inner peace and resilience that permeates every aspect of your life.

The benefits of morning workouts extend far beyond the gym. It is They energize your day, sharpen your focus, nourish the body, mind, and spirit, and leave you feeling invigorated. By embracing the transformative power of exercise, you embark on a journey of self-discovery and empowerment, unlocking your full potential and embracing each day with renewed vitality and purpose. Experience the difference—wake up early, work out, and reap the rewards.

SPEED
UP
READING

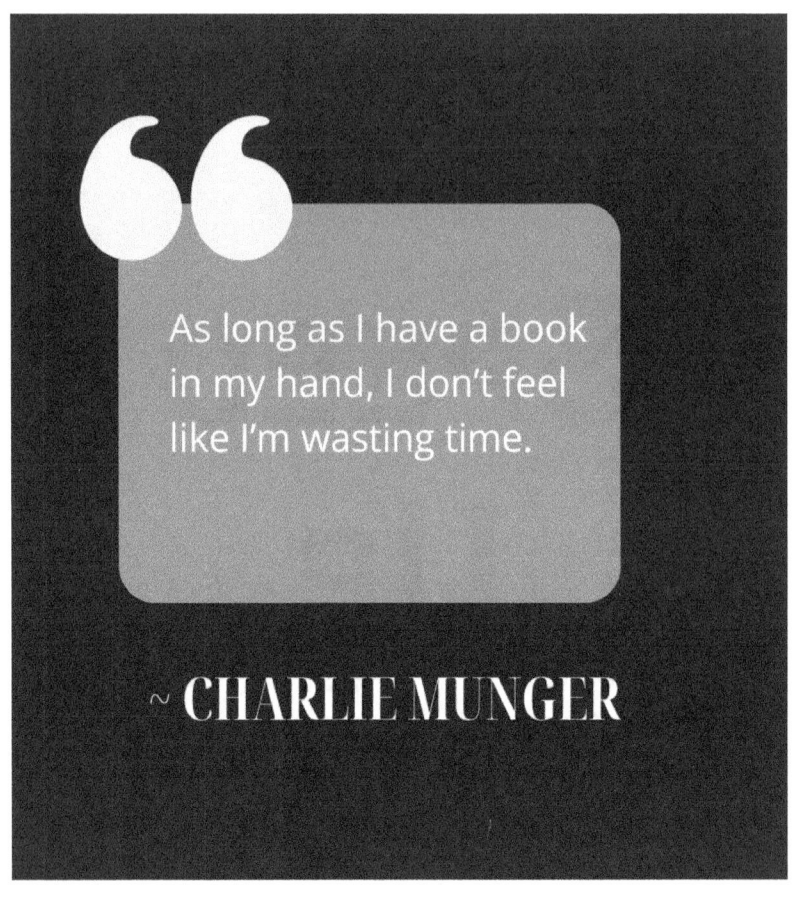

> As long as I have a book in my hand, I don't feel like I'm wasting time.
>
> ~ CHARLIE MUNGER

At 42 years old, reflecting on my journey as I write this book, I realize that the past two years have been a period of profound growth. In this relatively short span, I've devoured over 100 books—an achievement that has enriched my life a hundredfold compared to the past four decades.

Like many, I faced the question of how to cultivate a reading habit. Despite numerous attempts, I found myself faltering, unable to progress beyond a few lines before surrendering to drowsiness. Books seemed to possess a sedative effect similar to sleeping pills, upsetting my efforts to delve into their pages.

However, amidst these struggles, a steadfast desire to embrace reading persisted within me. And for good reason—ask any wise individual about their habits, and you'll find that 90% of them gave credit of their wisdom and growth to books.

In today's digital age, the allure of social media and video content threatens to overshadow the transformative power of reading. I've witnessed firsthand how children, once avid readers, have abandoned books in favor of mobile screens.

Reading habits are dying. We're surrounded by lots of ways to have fun and learn. Social media sites like Instagram, YouTube, and TikTok let people share all kinds of stuff. Some folks show off their cooking skills with yummy dishes from all over. Others take us on trips to faraway places with cool pictures and videos.

These platforms also let people give us a peek into their daily lives. They might show us around their homes or even their bathrooms, sharing tips and tricks along the way. It's a fun way to see how different people live and get some ideas for ourselves.

But with so much out there, it's good to remember to pick what's helpful and interesting to us. While these sites can be entertaining, they can also be overwhelming if we spend too much time on them. By choosing wisely and focusing on what brings us joy and learning, we can make the most of the digital world while still staying grounded in real life.

However; you must read to get the personal life-altering experience. All these sites and apps are free to give fake news, fake health tips, and negativity. There is no control.

I strongly believe that in the current world, the only medium that makes you think better is books. Real physical books or Digital books on reading platforms like Kindle.

There is a saying, *"Your education starts after your graduation"* one of them is books.

My journey into reading began two years ago with a borrowed copy of "Your Money or Your Life" by Vicki Robin—a finance book advocating early retirement. Rather than completing the book, I committed myself to a daily reading routine. Setting aside the hours between 6:30 AM and 7:30 AM, I found solace on the leftmost corner of my living room couch—a deliberate choice to foster the ideal environment for change.

With patience and persistence, I started small, progressing from one page to the next. Each day brought incremental victories, concluding in the completion of my first book within a month—an achievement that boosted my confidence and encouraged me forward.

This little victory gave me the confidence. I took another book and continued the same method; I did this every day. Yes, unwavering in my commitment, even on weekends, holidays, and sick days. Soon, books became my morning companions. I woke up with books as they gave me renewed energy and purpose. After this, I started buying physical books as this is an investment in my education.

I never thought I would ever adopt reading as a habit. I got it because I read what fascinated me. As my reading journey unfolded, my interests expanded beyond self-help and finance to include a diverse range of subjects. Encountering "Almanac of Naval Ravikant," I was captivated by its breadth of wisdom; I was amazed at how this tiny book contains lifelong lessons, spanning investments, philosophy, mathematics, and more.

One profound lesson I gathered from Naval Ravikant's teachings was the concept that *"Humans are multi-variant.'* They can do multiple things. Why is Elon Musk involved in launching rockets, and neuroscience while he is already super rich in electric cars?

Why Bill Gates talks about ecology, and covid when he is already super rich in Information Technology?

All the veterans understand they are multi-variant. They learn new things which are unrelated to what they are primarily doing. These in-depth details opened a new horizon in my life. I started reading microeconomics, personation, philosophy, memoirs, and selling; even now, I started reading palmistry.

I am sure the rest of my life will never be bored of reading. I am not just reading, but also learning new things every day. In essence, reading offers a path to empowerment—a means of exercising both body and mind, independent of external influences. As we navigate the complexities of life, let us not resign ourselves to passive observers but embrace the transformative potential of literature.

Have you ever thought why you are addicted to mobile phones or TV and keep surfing all videos, shorts, Insta, etc., for hours when you are low?

You want to escape from the current world. You think these little pleasures reduce your pressure. But it happens in reverse. You are adding more pressure to the current situation. All these activities are pulling into someone's thoughts, and you can't think about your next action and are stuck in a hamster wheel.

In contrast to the mindless scrolling and video consumption that often accompany moments of low mood, reading emerged as a powerful remedy—an invitation to engage with new ideas and perspectives. Rather than seeking escape, reading invited contemplation and creativity, fostering a deeper connection with oneself and the world.

This is like giving a contract to someone to do a workout on behalf of you to reduce your weight.

The result is the other person getting into shape, and you are gaining weight. This makes you feel guilty and depressed more as you see no improvements in your mind and body.

In contrast, if you apply reading in the same situation when you are low or to get motivated, it unfolds a new idea, and changes to do your next course of action. It makes your creativity or develop new ideas as a human being instead of just an individual. It's like you are working out on your body and mind instead of outsourcing to someone. This makes a big leap in your life.

We need to understand human life is not growing your kids, helping your wife or husband in the kitchen, working like a dog, and longing for retirement day. After retirement, they suffer from chronic diseases and die.

Human life is not merely a cycle of mundane routines and eventual decline. It is an opportunity for growth, discovery, and continuous learning. So, let us seize the days of our vitality, embarking on the exhilarating journey of reading and self-discovery.

Make use of the days when you are active. Put yourself in different tracks, Read, and Learn.

In closing, I echo the sentiments of Charlie Munger: "Read, read, read"—for within the pages of a book lies the key to unlocking the boundless potential of the human mind.

I don't have more to say….

SPEED UP WRITING

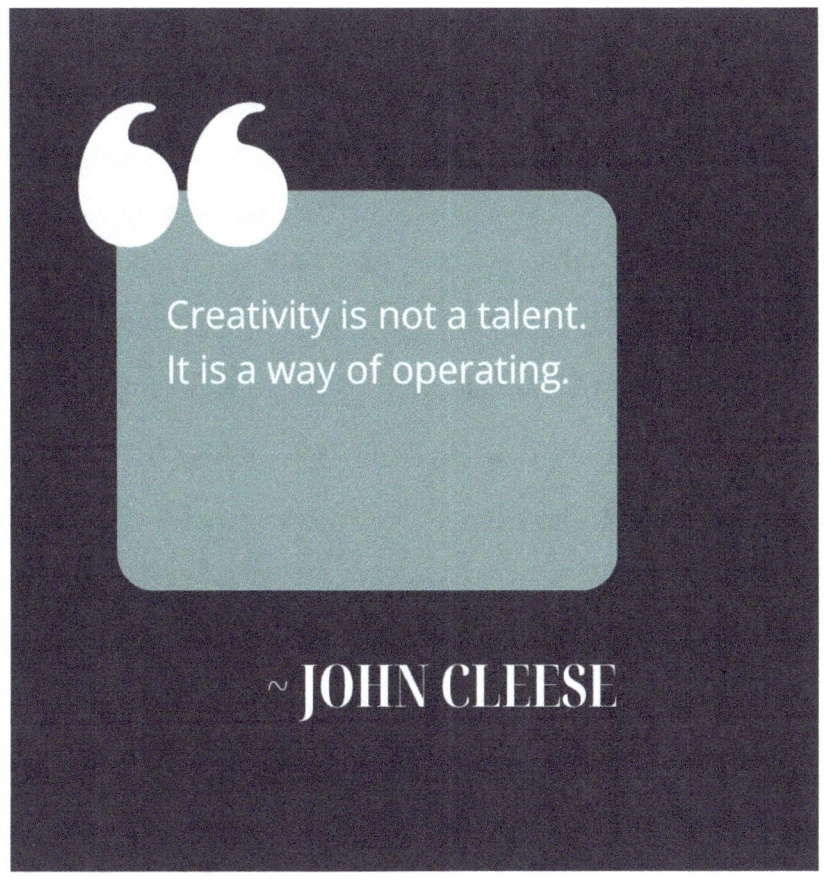

> Creativity is not a talent.
> It is a way of operating.

~ JOHN CLEESE

Writing is almost endangered in the current world. In an era dominated by digital communication, the art of handwriting is gradually fading into obscurity. Once considered an essential skill, the act of longhand writing now seems reserved for formal documents and nostalgic memories. The rise of technology has transformed the landscape of communication, consigning pen and paper to the lands of ancient times.

The declining practice of writing longhand is particularly evident among today's youth. Children, once tasked with filling notebooks with meticulous handwriting, now navigate virtual landscapes on laptops and tablets. The attraction of digital platforms, with their instant satisfaction and multimedia capabilities, has replaced the physical experience of putting pen to paper.

Adults stopped writing other than signing bank checks or restaurant bills. I don't remember any other place we write. Some people write journals every day to put their thoughts on everything from the heart. But writing is more than that.

However, amidst the appeal of keyboards and touchscreens, the importance of writing remains undiminished. Numerous studies underscore the cognitive benefits of handwriting, suggesting that the act of physically forming letters stimulates neural pathways associated with memory and comprehension. Research published in the journal Psychological Science indicates that students who take notes by hand tend to retain information more effectively than those who type.

In his book "Show Your Work," Austin Kleon commends the virtues of handwritten writing as a pioneer in digital composition. Kleon's creative process begins with the instinctive act of scribbling ideas longhand, striking and rewriting everything in a notebook and pen. Allowing thoughts to flow freely without the constraints of technology. Then he redoes the same on his computer. This approach, he argues, fosters a deeper connection with one's thoughts and ideas, laying the groundwork for more refined digital output.

Also, he divides his office space into analog and digital. Analog is to write physically whatever pops into his mind and complete it. Then, digitally, he typed the refined parts from his original manuscript.

However, the act of writing can be daunting for many. Despite consuming volumes of literature, some find themselves paralyzed when faced with a blank page. I know to get start writing is difficult. Some people read 100s of books and can't pen down even a single word. It's because we slide down this practice and little laziness. But this is a precious art; I encountered it many times.

Yet, the power of writing transcends mere communication. A handwritten note, crafted with sincerity and thoughtfulness, possesses a profound impact. Last Christmas, I gifted my daughter's school bus driver with a handwritten thank-you note alongside a small token of appreciation. Not a greeting card and my signature. It was a plain white paper and few words. Nothing fancy... The response was overwhelming—a testament to the enduring power of the written word. I got a return post from her about thanks for the gift and specifically about the thanks note I gave. My daughter and I are super happy; that's the power of writing. I am sure she will keep that piece of paper forever.

Reading a lot eventually ends up in writing. But we must give up the laziness on this. I am not saying you must write a book. But use it wherever possible in daily life.

The integration of writing into daily life need not be magnificent. A simple handwritten letter to an old friend can rekindle connections lost to time. The old practices always have value in this world. These timeless practices, from yoga to writing, hold intrinsic value in a world increasingly driven by fleeting trends.

But why do I write? Why do I immerse myself in the wisdom of literature? My aim is simple: to illuminate the beauty that surrounds us. Positivity, happiness, trust, and forgiveness—these virtues abound in our interactions with others. Through reading and writing, I navigate the maze of negativity, forging a path toward personal growth and transformation.

As an advocate of positive change, I often find myself sharing insights gleaned from literature with those I encounter. As a stranger, if you talk to me, I give at least 4 book references and a few words about the authors. I try to pass the messages to impact you positively. I normally do this whoever I meet But I can't do this for many people. I have no interest in social media sites to pass these messages Because these things are eradicated every decade. My thoughts won't stand for generations.

Yet, the fleeting nature of social media precludes the enduring impact of such messages. Platforms like Orkut, once buzzing with activity, now languish in obscurity—a testament to the briefness of digital landscapes. Now, Facebook, Instagram, and Twitter, do you think these stands for the next 50 years.

In "Who Will Cry When You Die" by Robin Sharma, three legacies endure beyond our lifetime: *the trees we plant, the children we raise, and the books we write.*

The power of the written word, is exemplified by timeless classics like 'Learn and Earn' by Peter Leech; 'Think and Grow Rich' by Napoleon Hill; 'Alchemist' by Paola Coelho, 'The Monk Who Sold His Ferrari' by Robin Sharma … all these are 20 to 40 years old books, but we can still utilize the knowledge even now. Your grandkids also can read and enjoy these. This is the power of writing art.

I am reading some books older than 50 years that still feel fresh and applicable in today's world. I am not here to peddle quick fixes or false promises. Life, I believe, is a journey—a journey marked by diligence, discipline, and unwavering commitment to personal growth. While my primary vocation sustains me, it is my quest to sow seeds of positivity that truly fuels my purpose.

I am not here to sell fake ideas, not how to get rich quickly, not sell pills to reduce weight quickly. **Quick, everything** is a myth. All the 4 habits I mentioned here are all about the life journey.

Life, ultimately, is about more than material wealth. True prosperity lies in the delicate balance of health, relationships, and financial stability. It is the pursuit of well-being—a journey guided by the principles of habit and discipline—that defines our existence. Yes, there is no shortcut in life. If it is, then it should be fake.

In essence, writing is not merely a means of communication but a form of self-expression—a conduit for ideas, emotions, and aspirations. As we navigate the complexities of modern existence, let us not overlook the transformative potential of the written word. For within its strokes and curves lies the power to inspire, to connect, and to illuminate the human experience.

I have a primary job to feed my family. All my needs are satisfied by the job. My intention is to pass the positivity which impacts your life. We need to step up on our laziness and put ourselves on track to improve our body, mind, and soul.

Life is not about what you like to do. It's about what you must do. There is a difference between well off and well-being.

Well off is being rich in terms of money. Money can't solve all your problems, but it solves your money problem. It buys you freedom, which is very important.

But well-being enriches your life. It boosts your health, relationships, and money. We must balance all these three. One can't help another if it is off-track. To keep all these, you need the right habits and discipline.